AUSTRALIA
the culture

Erinn Banting

A Bobbie Kalman Book

The Lands, Peoples, and Cultures Series

Crabtree Publishing Company

www.crabtreebooks.com

The Lands, Peoples, and Cultures Series

Created by Bobbie Kalman

Coordinating editor
Ellen Rodger

Project editor
Carrie Gleason

Production coordinator
Rosie Gowsell

Project development, photo research, design, and editing
First Folio Resource Group, Inc.
  Erinn Banting
  Tom Dart
  Söğüt Y. Güleç
  Claire Milne
  Jaimie Nathan
  Debbie Smith

Prepress and printing
Worzalla Publishing Company

Consultants
Jamie Breadmore; Amanda Burdon; Frank Povah, The Busy Boordy

Photographs
AP Photo/Rob Griffith: p. 11 (top); Art Resource/Tate Gallery, London: p. 25 (left); Australia Tourism Commission: p. 8, p. 12 (bottom), p. 20 (bottom); Bill Bachman: p. 3, p. 7 (left), p. 9 (top), p. 11 (bottom), p. 12 (top), p. 13 (bottom), p. 14 (both), p. 15 (bottom), p. 16 (both), p. 17 (both), p. 19 (bottom), p. 21 (top), p. 24 (top), p. 26 (bottom), p. 28 (top); P. Brylak/Photo Researchers: p. 5 (bottom); Corbis/Magma Photo News, Inc./ AFP: p. 29 (right); Corbis/Magma Photo News, Inc./Bettmann: p. 18 (left); Corbis/Magma Photo News, Inc./Pam Gardner: p. 6 (left); Corbis/Magma Photo News, Inc./Mitchell Gerber: p. 29 (left); Corbis/Magma Photo News, Inc./Dave G. Houser: p. 22, p. 25 (right); Corbis/Magma Photo News, Inc./Robbie Jack: p. 21 (bottom); Corbis/Magma Photo News, Inc./ Wolfgang Kaehler: cover; Corbis/Magma Photo News, Inc./ Reuters NewMedia Inc.: p. 19 (top), p. 28 (bottom); Corbis/ Magma Photo News, Inc./Penny Tweedie: p. 20 (top); Nancy Durrell McKenna/Hutchison Library: p. 27; Paul Dymond: p. 6 (right), p. 18 (right); Jean-Paul Ferrero/AUSCAPE: p. 9 (bottom), p. 10 (bottom), p. 15 (top); Private Collection: p. 24 (bottom); Michael James/Photo Researchers: title page; Michael Jensen/AUSCAPE: p. 4 (bottom), p. 13 (top); Jean-Marc LaRoque/AUSCAPE: p. 4 (top), p. 10 (top), p. 26 (top); Reg Morrison/AUSCAPE: p. 5 (top); Andre Singer/Hutchison Library: p. 7 (right); Penny Tweedie/Panos Pictures: p. 23

Illustrations
Dianne Eastman: icon
Kristi Frost: pp. 30–31
David Wysotski, Allure Illustrations: back cover

Cover: The Sydney Opera House is one of Australia's best-known landmarks because of its roof, which looks like a ship's sails. Inside the opera house are more than 1,000 rooms where people watch operas, concerts, plays, art exhibitions, and films.

Title page: Aboriginals dressed in grass skirts and ceremonial paint dance at a *corroboree* in the northeastern state of Queensland. *Corroborees* mark special events and give thanks to the Aboriginals' ancestors.

Icon: Boomerangs, which were first made by Aboriginals and used for hunting, appear at the head of each section. Many boomerangs are carved and brightly painted.

Back cover: When baby kangaroos, or joeys, are born, they are the size of a bean. Joeys spend 33 weeks inside their mother's pouches, by which time they are too big to be carried around.

Published by
Crabtree Publishing Company

PMB 16A,	612 Welland Avenue	73 Lime Walk
350 Fifth Avenue	St. Catharines	Headington
Suite 3308	Ontario, Canada	Oxford OX3 7AD
New York	L2M 5V6	United Kingdom
N.Y. 10118		

Cataloging in Publication Data
Banting, Erinn.
  Australia. The culture / Erinn Banting.
    p. cm. -- (Lands, peoples, and cultures series)
Includes index.
Summary: Text and photos show how Australians celebrate holidays and festivals, using art, music, and dance.
  ISBN 0-7787-9345-1 (RLB) -- ISBN 0-7787-9713-9 (pbk.)
  1. Australia--Civilization--Juvenile literature. 2. Australia--Social life and customs--Juvenile literature. [1. Australia--Civilization. 2. Australia--Social life and customs.] I. Title. II. Series.
DU107 .B36 2003
994--dc21
                                    2002013731
                                         LC

Contents

Many cultures into one

Australia is the smallest continent in the world and the only continent made up of just one country. The Aboriginals were the earliest known people to live there. Scientists believe they arrived from Asia at least 60,000 years ago. Another group of people, the Torres Strait Islanders, came nearly 10,000 years ago from New Guinea, an island in the Pacific Ocean.

In 1788, British settlers landed on Australia's shores, bringing new customs and traditions. Since then, people from more than 200 countries, including Greece, Italy, China, Japan, and Lebanon, have moved to Australia. Their foods, art, music, stories, and religious customs have become part of Australia's culture. This mix of cultures has created art, music, and traditions that reflect the rugged beauty of Australia's land and the **diversity** of its people.

An Aboriginal artist from the Northern Territory used a style of art called dot painting to create this picture. Many dot paintings tell about the history of the Aboriginal people.

A large breakfast of baked beans, bacon, fried tomatoes, and eggs gives this rancher energy for his busy day herding cattle in the outback.

Three girls with elaborate headdresses prepare to perform at a Chinese New Year's celebration in Sydney, the capital of New South Wales. At Chinese New Year celebrations, people dance, sing, and sample traditional Chinese foods.

In Australia, people spend a lot of time at the beach swimming, surfing, or scuba diving. Water sports are such a large part of life in Australia that every year there are surf carnivals, where lifeguards, called lifesavers, compete in swimming, boating, and running races, and demonstrate their lifesaving skills.

The Dreaming

The Dreaming is central to the life of all Aboriginals. It consists of stories about their **ancestors**, who were present during the Dreamtime, when Aboriginals believe the world was created. Beings in the Dreamtime created mountains, valleys, oceans, deserts, and the seasons, then they were absorbed into the land where they continue to live. Different groups of Aboriginals celebrate different Dreamtime beings and the **sacred** sites where they make their home.

Dancers wearing traditional costumes perform at the Laura Festival, which celebrates the culture and history of Australia's Aboriginals and Torres Strait Islanders.

Scattered across the Northern Territory are giant boulders that Aboriginals believe are eggs laid by the Rainbow Serpent.

The Supreme Creator

Although many of the Aboriginals' beliefs vary, there are similarities from group to group. Almost all groups believe in a Supreme Creator who filled the world with plants, animals, and humans after the work of the Dreamtime beings was done. Some groups give the Supreme Creator different names, such as Byamee and Nargacork. Other groups believe that certain Dreamtime beings are the Supreme Creator. In northern Australia, for example, Aboriginals believe that the Rainbow Serpent is the Supreme Creator.

Sneaky creatures

Most beings from the Dreamtime are kind and generous, but some are considered wicked and evil. The Net-nets are naughty, invisible spirits that hide objects to confuse people. The Yuurii, or "hairymen," are usually kind spirits, but they punish people for their wrongdoings by biting them with their big teeth, throwing stones at them, or kidnapping them.

Totems

Totems are symbols, such as plants, animals, ancestors, or Dreamtime beings, that are believed to protect Aboriginals from harm. Each person has a totem, and each Aboriginal group has one or more totems that its members take care of. For example, if a group's totem is a kangaroo, members of the group do not harm kangaroos or eat kangaroo meat. They show kangaroos in their art and sing about them in their music. Special ceremonies, called *corroborees*, are held to honor kangaroos.

Elders

Corroborees are held for other occasions, such as giving thanks, asking for rain, welcoming a person into adulthood, or marking someone's death. Elders, who are the most knowledgeable and respected members of the group, lead the *corroborees*. Some elders, who are thought to have special powers, are called clever-men and clever-women. It is believed that they can communicate with Dreamtime creatures by going into a trance or state in which they are in touch with their Dreaming. Clever-men and clever-women endure painful physical **rituals** to enter this state, such as scarring their bodies.

An Arrernte man, from central Australia, prepares to lead an initiation ceremony, which marks a boy's passage into adulthood.

Many Aboriginal people have adopted Christianity as part of their beliefs. In this Aboriginal church in the Northern Territory, stories from the Bible are painted in traditional Aboriginal styles.

Bipotaim

The Torres Strait Islanders live on a group of islands in the Torres Strait, off the northeast coast of Australia, and on the mainland. Their traditional religion is Bipotaim. Like the Aboriginal belief in the Dreaming, Bipotaim is based on a deep respect for ancestors and for the land. Bipotaim differs from the Dreaming because there is a strong belief in the **supernatural** and in magic, which people can use for good or evil. According to Bipotaim, magic can be found in natural objects and places, such as trees or areas of land, and in objects that people make, such as masks or carvings.

The influence of Bipotaim can still be seen in the culture of the Torres Strait Islanders, although most Islanders are now Christians. Christians believe there is one God, and they worship his son, Jesus Christ. Jesus' teachings are written in a part of the Bible called the New Testament.

Anglicanism and Roman Catholicism, which are both **denominations** of Christianity, are the main religions in Australia. Australians also follow other faiths, such as Judaism, Islam, Buddhism, and Greek Orthodoxy. People from these religions celebrate many holidays and events throughout the year.

Christmas

Christmas, on December 25, celebrates the birth of Jesus Christ. Australians decorate their homes with lights and ornaments hung from pine trees or eucalyptus branches. Instead of singing the usual words to "The Twelve Days of Christmas," Australians sing of "twelve koalas clowning, eleven lizards leaping, ten dingoes dancing, nine numbats knitting, eight quokkas cooking, seven mice a-marching, six penguins peeping, five crocodiles, four pelicans, three lorikeets, two wallabies, and a bellbird in a flame tree." Because Christmas in Australia takes place during the summer, "Jingle Bells" has special lyrics: "Jingle bells, jingle bells, jingle all the way! Christmas in Australia on a scorching summer's day, hey!"

A fine Christmas meal

On Christmas Day, most Australian families eat a traditional dinner, with turkey or a roast lamb, potatoes, and gravy. Other people have seafood barbecues. Australians also eat special Christmas treats. Christmas damper is a type of homemade bread in the shape of a star or Christmas tree. It is served with butter, jam, honey, or syrup. White Christmas is made with a rice cereal called Rice Bubbles, as well as mixed fruit, coconut, icing sugar, powdered milk, vanilla, and copha, which is like shortening.

Christmas in Australia is in the summer, so Santa Claus is sometimes seen on the beach, swimming, surfing, or riding in a speedboat.

On religious holidays such as Christmas and Easter, this church in Western Australia fills with people who come to celebrate, worship, and give thanks.

Boxing Day

December 26 is Boxing Day. This holiday gets its name because wealthy people in England used to give their servants a small box of money, clothing, or another gift as a bonus on the day after Christmas.

Throughout Australia, many special events take place on Boxing Day. One of the most exciting sporting matches of the year, the Boxing Day Cricket Test, is held in Melbourne, in the southeast. It begins on December 26 and lasts five days. Cricket is similar to baseball, but players do not run around the bases. Instead, they run between wickets at opposite ends of the field. In Sydney, also in the southeast, tens of thousands of people gather to watch the start of the Sydney-to-Hobart Yacht Race, which runs down the east coast to Tasmania.

The 630-mile (1,014-kilometer) Sydney-to-Hobart Yacht Race first took place in 1945, and now has participants from all over Australia, England, Ireland, Scotland, Japan, New Zealand, and the United States.

Easter

Easter marks the death of Jesus Christ and his return to life. Christians celebrate Easter by going to church for a special service, or Mass. Children also hunt for Easter eggs and candies. Australians had a long tradition of eating chocolate Easter bunnies, as North Americans do, but today they are encouraged to buy Easter bilbies instead. A bilby is a type of bandicoot, with long ears like a rabbit, that is found only in Australia. The chocolate bunnies are a reminder of the damage large numbers of rabbits have caused Australia's landscape.

A brother and sister are excited to eat their chocolate Easter bilbies.

Chinese New Year celebrations begin on the first full moon of the new year and last fifteen days. Traditionally, the holiday was marked with a religious celebration in which people gave thanks to their family and ancestors, the spirits of their household, and the earth and heavens. Today, in Sydney, the Chinese New Year is marked by a large parade.

Fun festivals

January 26, Australia Day, remembers the landing of the first British settlers in Australia. Actors in costumes re-enact the settlers' arrival in **replicas** of the first ships. People join in the national anthem at a special ceremony, and in the evening there is a "sky show," or fireworks display. Many newcomers to Australia also become citizens in ceremonies across the country on Australia Day.

Veterans, or people who fought in wars for their country, march at an ANZAC Day parade in Sydney.

This ram, or male sheep, has just won first place in a competition for the softest and fullest fleece, or wool.

ANZAC Day

ANZAC Day is celebrated on April 25 in Australia and in the neighboring country of New Zealand. ANZAC stands for the Australian and New Zealand Army Corps. On ANZAC Day, Australians and New Zealanders remember the people who fought in wars for their countries. They hold services, which often begin at dawn, with prayers, speeches, the laying of wreaths on soldiers' tombstones and public monuments, a minute of silence, and bugle calls.

Royal agricultural shows

Royal agricultural shows, or "show days," are held throughout Australia. At the agricultural shows, farmers, **breeders**, and spectators come from different regions to learn about new farming equipment, to display their crops and animals, and to compete in events. Farmers win prizes for having the largest fruit, vegetable, or animal. Competitions, such as pig and sheep races and obstacle courses run by sheep dogs, test animals' skills and obedience. Wood choppers try to be the first to chop through thick logs. Young people receive awards too. The Rural Achievers Award honors a young person who is involved in agriculture in his or her community.

This group celebrates the Moomba Festival wearing traditional costumes from Bosnia, the European country where their ancestors lived.

The Moomba Festival

Each March, Melbourne hosts the Moomba Festival. This festival gives people from different backgrounds a chance to share their culture with one another. There are carnival rides, fireworks displays, and a **tram** parade, which features trams from different times in history. A highlight of the Moomba Festival are the "Moomba masters," water-skiers and **wake-boarders** who perform incredible stunts.

The Torres Strait Cultural Festival celebrates the costumes, dances, songs, food, and arts of the Torres Strait Islanders. A dancer, wearing a traditional headdress, performs at the festival, which is held each year on Thursday Island.

Events in the outback

In the center of Australia is a vast area known as the outback, with endless deserts, odd rock formations, and enormous sheep and cattle ranches, or stations. Celebrations in the outback reflect the life and culture there. One of the most popular celebrations is the Coober Pedy Opal Festival, which is held in April. During the four-day festival, people watch sporting events and musical performances. They visit shops to see the rare **opals** that are mined in Coober Pedy, and take tours of the underground town. Most homes in Coober Pedy are built underground because the temperatures above ground are very hot during the day and very cold at night. Underground, the temperature is always a comfortable 77° Fahrenheit (25° Celsius).

The World Solar Challenge is another event held in the outback each year. Competitors from all over the world race their solar-powered cars for 1,864 miles (2,997 kilometers) through the desert, from Darwin, in the north, to Adelaide, in the south. The World Solar Challenge is the world's longest race of cars that are powered by the sun's energy.

Glendi

Glendi is a Greek festival held in Adelaide in March to celebrate Greek Independence Day. Australia has the largest Greek population outside Greece itself, and *Glendi* gives the community a chance to celebrate its Greek-Australian heritage. In Greek, *glendi* means "celebration." At the festival, people sample foods from different regions of Greece, learn about these regions, and see traditional costumes and dances. There is also an exhibition of life-sized statues of athletes competing in ancient Greek sports, such as wrestling, **javelin** throwing, and **discus**.

The fastest cars in the World Solar Challenge travel at speeds of more than 55 miles (90 kilometres) per hour, taking just over 32 hours to complete the race. Much slower cars travel at average speeds of 22 miles (35 kilometers) per hour, taking more than 89 hours to complete the race.

Strange Fruit, a theater group that stands on top of long flexible poles, performs during the Melbourne International Festival of the Arts. Strange Fruit uses dance, mime, and poetry in their performances.

"Barbies" and other tucker

Australia's weather is nice year-round, so families often cook and eat outdoors at barbecues, or "barbies." Many people in the outback also cook their food, or "tucker," over an open flame. "Tucker" originally referred to food that people in the outback ate. Today, it usually refers to any traditional Australian dish. Other foods that are popular in Australia have come from England, Greece, Italy, and Asian countries, such as China, Japan, and Thailand.

Many meals

"Brekkie," or breakfast, used to be the largest meal of the day for many Australians. Farmers drank tea or coffee and ate toast, eggs, and "snags" or "bangers," which are types of sausages, to give them energy for the day. Some people even ate baked beans, spaghetti, ground beef on toast, or a grilled lamb chop. Many Australians still eat a large breakfast, but others prefer cereal, a muffin or toast, and juice, tea, or coffee. For lunch, people eat "sangers," or sandwiches, fish and chips, meat pies, sausage rolls, and fresh fruit and vegetables. Supper commonly includes potatoes, beef, lamb, or "chook," which is what Australians call chicken.

Barbecued hamburgers, hotdogs, and sausages make a tasty lunch at the Mansfield Cup Picnic Races. The Mansfield Cup is a horse race that is held in Victoria each year.

Lamingtons, which are sponge cakes covered in chocolate and coconut, are part of an afternoon snack called tea. The tradition of having tea comes from England.

"Barbies"

People in Australia grill almost everything. Meat, vegetables, and fish are some of the most common foods to "slap on the barbie." Australians flavor their grilled food with **marinades** and sauces, and they cook with wood chips, instead of charcoal, as many North Americans do, to give the food a smoky flavor. Australians do not only barbecue at home; some restaurants also have outdoor grills where customers prepare their own meals. Beaches, parks, and picnic areas also have grills that picnickers use.

Markets that sell silver bream, barramundi, and other fresh fish caught off the coasts are common in Australia's towns and cities.

Seafood

More than 1,500 types of edible fish, or fish that is safe to eat, live in Australia's waters, so Australians eat a lot of seafood. Some favorites are oysters, crayfish, and the Moreton Bay bug. The Tasmanian crab, which can weigh up to 30 pounds (14 kilograms), is used in many dishes. The giant shellfish can be barbecued or added to stir fries, pasta dishes, and other foods.

Vegemite

In 1922, an Australian named Fred Walker asked the scientists in the food company he owned to create a nutritious snack. They invented Vegemite, a thick, salty, black spread that combines celery, onions, and other vegetables with yeast, which contains vitamin B. Vegemite immediately became popular. To this day, Australians spread Vegemite on bread, toast, and crackers instead of using peanut butter or jam.

Many Australians eat Vegemite every day, especially on their toast at breakfast.

One way to cook damper is in a pot hung over a campfire. While the food closer to the fire is cooking, the heat from the flame also cooks the damper.

Tucker in the outback

For hundreds of years, people in the outback have eaten foods that most people would find surprising, including lizards and bugs. Witchetty grubs resemble large caterpillars. When eaten raw, they taste like butter. When cooked in a frying pan with herbs, they taste like pork.

People camping in the outback usually prepare their food on an open fire. They cook damper in a pot over the fire or in the fire's ashes until the bread rises and is golden brown. They make billy tea by adding tea and eucalyptus leaves to water boiled in a camp can, or kettle, called a billy. More unusual items cooked over an open fire are snakes, turtles, eels, emus, and kangaroos. Kangaroo meat is now popular in many Australian cities. In some restaurants, people can order grilled kangaroo tail as their main dish.

Damper

Children throughout Australia eat damper during camping trips and as a special treat. You can make this tasty bread with an adult's help.

You will need:
2 cups (500 ml) flour
1/2 teaspoon (2 ml) salt
2 teaspoons (10 ml) sugar
1 teaspoon (5 ml) baking powder
1 tablespoon (15 ml) butter
1 cup (250 ml) milk or water (enough to make a soft dough)
butter, jam, honey, or syrup

What to do:
1. Mix the flour, salt, sugar, and baking powder together.
2. Add the butter and mix again.
3. Add the milk or water and knead with your hands.
4. Place on a baking tray, or mold into different shapes and put on a cookie sheet.
5. Bake at 350˚ Fahrenheit (180˚ Celsius) for 20 minutes or until brown.
6. Serve hot with butter, jam, honey, or syrup.

Witchetty grubs are not only used for food in the outback. Some Aboriginal groups give them to babies who are teething because the grubs' skin is very leathery.

Food on the Torres Strait Islands

The Torres Strait Islanders have traditional dishes that are not eaten anywhere else in Australia. Green turtles are often eaten during feasts, or celebrations. On the Torres Strait Islands, it is illegal for anyone who is not a Torres Strait Islander to hunt or kill green turtles. Another animal that is part of the Islanders' diet is the dugong, a large **mammal** that lives in the Pacific Ocean. Dugong meat is prepared using a method called *kopmari*. The meat is cooked on stones that have been heated for hours. *Sop-sop*, which is made from yams and pumpkins cooked with coconut cream, is often served with green turtle and dugong.

Sweets and treats

Children in Australia eat many types of candy bars and sweets, just like children in North America. In Australia, candies and lollipops are called "lollies." Popsicles, which children enjoy on hot days, are called "icy poles." Big M is a brand of milk that is flavored to taste like all sorts of things, including chocolate, mint, and oranges.

Vegetables such as red peppers, onions, celery, and cucumber, which are grown throughout Australia, are being used to make a salad.

Two girls enjoy Big Ms on their way home from school. Can you tell which flavors the girls are drinking?

Sing along and dance!

Australian music and dance are known around the world. Opera singers, such as Dame Nellie Melba (1859–1931), drew worldwide attention to Australia and its music during the late 1800s. Dame Melba was so popular that a French chef, Auguste Escoffier, named a dessert after her — *pêche Melba*, or peach Melba. Melba toast is also named after her.

Dame Melba's name was originally Helen Porter Mitchell, but she changed it to Melba because she loved Melbourne so much.

Early music

Songs sung at *corroborees* are the oldest form of music in Australia. Some of these songs are hundreds of verses long and tell stories of the Dreaming. Songlines are types of songs that tell of the journey of Dreamtime spirits as they created Australia's landscape. The songs describe the landscape in such detail that Aboriginals use them instead of maps to guide them through the desert. Songlines also teach people the laws by which they should live.

Many songs and chants sung by the Torres Strait Islanders are only a few words long. They tell about the Islanders' ancestors, and are used in rituals and spells.

Traditional instruments

Traditional instruments used by Aboriginals and Torres Strait Islanders are now played by other Australian musicians, including clap sticks, clubs, and boomerangs, which are tapped together. The *didgeridoo* is a long instrument that makes a droning sound which no other instrument can produce. Traditionally, it was made from eucalyptus branches that termites hollowed out. Today, it is made from a hollow wooden tube.

*Musicians who play the **didgeridoo** must be able to do circular breathing, which means that they do not stop to breathe between notes. Instead, they take one long breath, blow into the instrument, and while blowing air out through their mouth, they suck air in through their nose. That way, they never have to stop playing.*

Bush music

English, Irish, Scottish, and American music have influenced Australian folk music. Bush music is a type of quick, country music played on fiddles, tin whistles, banjos, and other instruments brought from Britain and the United States. The Bushwackers are a popular bush band whose songs often describe life in Australia.

Waltzing Matilda

"Waltzing Matilda, waltzing Matilda,
Who'll come a-waltzing Matilda with me?"
And he sang as he watched
and waited till his billy boiled,
"Who'll come a-waltzing Matilda with me?"

"Waltzing Matilda" is considered by some people to be Australia's unofficial national anthem. It was written by Andrew "Banjo" Paterson in the 1890s about a "swagman," or drifter, who steals a "jumbuck," or sheep. To avoid being arrested, he drowns himself in a "billabong," or pool of water. Some people think that the words in the song have no meaning, but they are actually terms that were widely used in Australia in the late 1800s. In the chorus, for example, "Matilda" refers to the swagman's bed roll, and to "go waltzing Matilda" means to go on the road with a bed roll on your back.

Peter Garrett, the lead singer of Midnight Oil, sings "Beds are Burning" during the closing ceremonies for the 2000 Olympics, which were held in Sydney. The "Sorry" on his shirt is an apology to Aboriginals for the crimes committed against them by the government.

Popular music

Many Australian singers have enjoyed success in other countries. Some groups, including Midnight Oil, play *didgeridoos* and other traditional instruments. They also use their pop music to teach people about Australia. Midnight Oil's song "Beds Are Burning," for example, tells about the government taking land from the Aboriginals.

Musicians playing guitars and drums perform a bush song at a festival in Melbourne.

Yothu Yindi

Yothu Yindi, which means "child and mother," is a group made of Aboriginal and non-Aboriginal musicians. They have created their own sound by blending rock music with Aboriginal music played on modern and traditional instruments. Yothu Yindi's songs focus on issues that concern Aboriginals, such as their relationship with the land and land rights. "Treaty," for example, tells about the government's failure to give land back to the Aboriginals.

Aboriginal dances

Many Aboriginal dances accompany traditional songs that honor a group's totem or a Dreamtime creature. Performers wear traditional costumes, such as skirts made from grasses, small aprons decorated with belts of human hair, headbands, neckbands, and nosepegs. Nosepegs are pieces of bone, wood, **reeds**, or quills from a prickly animal called an echidna that are passed through a hole pierced in the nose. Some dances imitate the movements of animals. Others tell ancient stories about Dreamtime beings creating the land. In these dances, performers imitate the movements of the Dreamtime creatures.

Aboriginal women perform a dance at a **corroboree** *in Western Australia.*

Dancers from the Torres Strait Islands wear accessories called dance machines on their wrists. When this dancer moves his wrist in a certain way, it looks as if his sailboat dance machine is bobbing through the water.

Dances in the Torres Strait

Dances on the Torres Strait Islands mark everything from family celebrations to historical events. Traditionally, dancers wore masks and headdresses made from the shells of green turtles. Today, the masks are made of wood, **fibers**, and the shells of smaller animals. The best-known headdress is the u-shaped *deri*, which is made from white feathers. It is the symbol of the Torres Strait Islanders and appears on their flag. Dance machines are other accessories used in traditional dances to represent totems, natural landmarks, or people. They are often models of stars, flowers, or sea animals.

Dances from around the world

Irish and Scottish people brought Celtic dances, such as step dances, to Australia. Step dancers move their feet very quickly on the spot while keeping their arms by their sides. Australia's Greek and Chinese communities perform their traditional dances at festivals and special events. Other forms of dance have been created in Australia. Tap Dogs is a dance troupe that performs a loud kind of tap dance in heavy work boots on a set that looks like a construction site.

People take dance lessons in a courtyard in Melbourne.

The cast of Tap Dogs creates a stomping rhythm as they dance down bleachers in their heavy boots.

Art, past and present

Throughout Australia's history, artists have told stories and described their country's landscape in their work. Aboriginals used interesting patterns and designs to create the first paintings of people, animals, and Dreamtime creatures. Paintings were traditionally done on cave walls, rocks, branches, sand, and people's bodies.

Paintings in caves and on canvas

Some of Australia's cave paintings and rock engravings are more than 25,000 years old. In Kakadu National Park, in the Northern Territory, paintings show Australia's animals, such as kangaroos, and historical events, such as the arrival of the British. Some cave painting sites are kept secret because Aboriginals consider them sacred.

Traditionally, Aboriginal artists also painted on the flat bark of the stringybark tree. Many of today's artists continue this artform using yellow, black, and white paints made from clay, charcoal, and a mineral called ocher. Other artists paint in traditional styles on canvas. Like some paintings done in caves, they use the x-ray style. In x-ray paintings, bones and organs are shown. Other artists create dot paintings, which use thousands of colored dots to form images.

(right) Aboriginals visit ancient sites, such as the cave shelters at Arnhem Land, in central Australia, to see cave paintings that tell stories about the Dreaming.

(below) Bark paintings, woven rugs, and baskets stand on display at an art fair in Arnhem Land.

Boomerangs

Boomerangs were invented by Aboriginals thousands of years ago. They are often decorated in traditional styles of painting, such as the x-ray and dot styles. There are many kinds of boomerangs. One type is used for hunting. It is 2 feet (0.6 meters) long, with a slight curve at one end and a sharp edge at the other. Another type is used for fun and in competitions. It weighs less than the hunting boomerang, is more curved, and comes back to the person who throws it.

The Heidelberg School

By the 1800s, Australians were being influenced by European styles of art, such as Impressionism. Impressionism is a style of painting that uses bright colors and blurry shapes to represent everyday objects. A group of artists called The Heidelberg School, named after the suburb of Melbourne where they worked, portrayed Australia's landscape and the daily life of ordinary people in the Impressionist style. Jane Sutherland's (1855–1928) painting *Daydream*, for example, uses bright colors and soft shapes to depict a woman who has fallen asleep in the sun while reading a book.

Each Aboriginal group uses its own style when decorating boomerangs and other crafts. These boomerangs and necklaces from Western Australia reflect the culture of the Pintupi people.

*A woman relaxing, like the woman in Jane Sutherland's painting **Daydream**, was a common subject in paintings from the late 1800s.*

Modern art

The outback and Australia's history have inspired the country's artists. *The Drover's Wife*, by Russell Drysdale (1912–1981), is a painting that conveys a feeling of loneliness, as it depicts a woman standing in a desolate, ugly landscape. *The Glenrowan Series*, by Sidney Nolan (1917–1992), is a series of paintings about Ned Kelly. Ned Kelly was a famous bushranger, or outlaw, who committed crimes in the late 1800s. One of the best known paintings in *The Glenrowan Series* is *Death of Constable Scanlon*, which depicts Ned Kelly as a hooded, dark figure, and a constable, whom he has shot, hanging upside down.

"The spirit of the place"

One of Australia's most famous artists, Albert Namatjira (1902–1959), was a member of the Aranda people. He used **watercolors** to show scenes from the outback, including sacred sites, and to capture what Aboriginals call "the spirit of the place," or the spirit of the area where

they live. In many of his canvases, he painted a species of eucalyptus tree called the ghost gum. These canvases include *A Painting of Ghost Gums* and *Valley Ghost Gums, MacDonnell Ranges*. Many of Namatjira's works of art were sold around the world. He gave all the money he earned to help the Aranda people.

The Living Desert

Outside the town of Broken Hill, in New South Wales, stand twelve enormous sculptures carved out of a type of rock called sandstone. The sculptures in the Living Desert represent Dreamtime creatures. They were the idea of American sculptor Lawrence Beck (1962–), who invited Australian artists, as well as artists from around the world, to work on the project.

(top) **In this painting from** The Glenrowan Series, *Sidney Nolan depicts outlaw Ned Kelly wearing his armor, which he and his gang made to protect themselves from gunfire.*

Language in Oz

It has been yonks since these mates from uni have had a good chin-wag. This is strine for "It has been a long time since these friends from university have had a good chat."

(top) Girls who immigrated to Australia from Vietnam chat in English with their new friends. At home, they speak Vietnamese with their families.

English is Australia's official language, but it is different than the English spoken in Britain or North America. Australians call their dialect, or version, of English "strine." Certain words are pronounced differently, and certain objects have different names. Some of these names are short forms. Instead of having barbecues, Australians have "barbies." Australians do not live in Australia; they live in "Oz." On birthdays, they give each other "pressies," not "presents."

In Australia	In North America
Ta.	Thanks.
No worries.	You're welcome.
G'day mate!	Good day, friend!
Beaut.	Terrific.
Crikey!	Gee! or Wow!
Dead set!	Really!
Knackered.	Tired.
Fussed.	Irritated or angry.

Languages from many countries

Many Australians who immigrated from countries around the world still speak their native languages as well as English. Among these languages are Chinese, Japanese, Greek, Italian, and French. Australians read books, watch television programs, and listen to radio stations in their native languages. In Australia, radio programs are broadcast in more than 52 languages.

Aboriginal languages

Long ago, more than 250 Aboriginal languages were spoken in Australia. Approximately 150 of those languages have been lost since the first British settlers arrived. Today, only about one-fifth of Aboriginals speak their native languages. Pitjantjatjara, which is spoken in the south-central deserts, is the most common Aboriginal language. There are 10,000 words in the language, which are made up from three vowels and seventeen consonants.

These children learn to speak both English and Pintupi at their school in Western Australia.

Ways of saying things

Aboriginal languages differ from one another, but they have some words in common. In many Aboriginal languages, *jina* means "foot" and *mala* means "hand." Some languages have many words for the same object. Pintupi, which is spoken in the Gibson Desert, in Western Australia, has eighteen words for "hole." Other languages have single words that translate into entire English sentences. In Tiwi, which is spoken on Bathurst and Melville Islands, in the north, the long word *yuwunimarriwayangirri* means "he sent them a message."

Aboriginal English

Until the 1970s, the government discouraged Aboriginals from speaking their native languages, and Aboriginal children were taught English instead. Today, many Aboriginal communities have bilingual schools and language centers where children learn both their native language and English. In other places, Aboriginals speak new dialects that combine English and Aboriginal languages. Kriol, for example, is an Aboriginal English language spoken across northern Australia.

In print, on stage, and on screen

Australia's first stories were Aboriginal tales about the creation of their country and the world. When colonists arrived from Britain, they began to tell their own stories about life in the wild outback. The spirit of adventure and the Australian landscape have also been the subject of plays, movies, and television programs that are watched around the world.

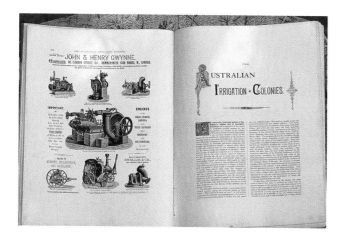

An almanac from the 1800s explains how to irrigate, or water, Australia's rugged terrain. Many early colonists turned to almanacs for information about farming and for accounts about other farmers' experiences.

Australia's first novel

The first Australian novel was *Quintus Servinton* by Henry Savery (1791–1842). Savery was a convict who wrote about life in a penal colony. Penal colonies were settlements where prisoners lived and were forced to do hard labor. Later novels and poems, called "bush ballads," told about life in the outback. Henry Lawson (1867–1922) was a poet who wrote about the loneliness and hardships of living in the bush.

Modern literature

Many of Australia's modern authors are popular around the world. Thomas Keneally (1935–) writes novels that are based mainly on history, with main characters who are in conflict with people in power. His novel *Schindler's Ark*, which was turned into the movie *Schindler's List*, tells of German factory owner Oskar Schindler who saved 1,300 Jews during **World War II**. Peter Carey (1943–) is a prize-winning author who was born in Australia and now lives in New York. His books include *Oscar and Lucinda* and *True History of the Kelly Gang*, about the bushranger Ned Kelly.

Thomas Keneally does research for a new novel in his study filled with books.

Oodgeroo Noonuccal

Oodgeroo Noonuccal (1920–1993) was an Aboriginal poet who wrote new works based on old Aboriginal poems, songs, myths, and legends. Her collection of poetry *We Are Going* was published in 1964. It was the first book ever published by an Aboriginal woman. Oodgeroo Noonuccal was known as Kath Walker until later in life when she began to use her Aboriginal name. She also painted, fought for Aboriginal rights, and started an educational center to teach Aboriginals and non-Aboriginals about Aboriginal culture.

To the movies!

Many popular movies, such as *Babe: Pig in the City*, *Mad Max 2*, and *Crocodile Dundee*, were filmed in Australia, and many popular actors were born there or have lived there. Mel Gibson, for example, was born in the United States but grew up in Australia. He starred in movies such as the *Lethal Weapon* series, the *Mad Max* series, and *Braveheart*.

In her shows, Dame Edna sings, dances, and makes fun of her audience.

Australian theater

Australian theater has gained attention since the 1970s. David Williamson is Australia's most performed playwright. He has written 26 plays and won many awards, including eleven Australian Writers' Guild Awards. Barry Humphries is an actor known for his one-person shows in which he plays the role of Dame Edna Everage, a character known for her outrageous costumes and sense of humor.

On TV

Australian television shows are often full of adventures and dangerous stunts. In *The Crocodile Hunter*, Steve and Terri Irwin teach people about Australia's remarkable wildlife by doing stunts such as wrestling crocodiles and capturing poisonous snakes. Not all shows are filled with tense moments in the wilderness. *Neighbors* is a popular soap opera about **suburban** life in Australia that is viewed by more than 120 million people around the world each day.

Nicole Kidman was born in Hawaii, but grew up in Australia where she became well known as an actress in Australian films and television. She has starred in movies such as **Eyes Wide Shut** *and* **Moulin Rouge**.

An Aboriginal tale

Aboriginal stories have traditionally been passed down **orally** from generation to generation. They have guided people in their lives and taught important lessons about how to treat others.

As Aboriginal peoples disappeared, so did many of their stories. Today, Aboriginals are writing down their tales so no more are lost. "The Firemakers" was first written down by a non-Aboriginal woman named Katherine Langloh Parker (1856–1940). She collected this story from the Yuwaaliyaay people, whose traditional lands are in New South Wales.

The firemakers

Long ago, when the ancestors roamed the earth, only the Supreme Creator knew how to make fire. The ancestors ate their food raw, or they dried it in the sun.

One day, Bootoolgah the crane was rubbing two sticks from a firestick tree together when she noticed a spark. "Look!" she exclaimed to Goonur the kangaroo rat, "Maybe if I rub these sticks together near that dried grass and bark, one spark may light a fire. Then, we would not have to eat our food raw or wait for it to dry in the sun."

Goonur was excited when he saw the small flame. "We must not tell anyone about the secrets of the firestick tree. We will cook our food where no one can see us, then hide one stick in our *comebee*, or sack, and the other among the scrub near our camp."

The next day, Bootoolgah and Goonur cooked their fish in the fire, and it was very tasty. When the other animals saw the leftovers back at the camp, they wondered why the crane and kangaroo rat's fish looked different than the fish they dried in the sun. Bootoolgah and Goonur insisted it was the same.

Each day, Bootoolgah and Goonur snuck away to cook their fish. The other animals noticed that their friends disappeared whenever they ate. Boolooral the night owl and Quarrian the parrot decided to follow Bootoolgah and Goonur to see where they went.

The next day, Boolooral and Quarrian watched as Bootoolgah and Goonur took one stick out of their *comebee* and the other stick from the scrub, and made a fire to cook their meal. Back at the camp, Boolooral and Quarrian told the others what they had seen.

The animals decided on a plan. They would hold the largest *corroboree* ever. While Bootoolgah and Goonur were being entertained, Beeargah the hawk would steal the sticks.

On the day of the *corroboree*, Bootoolgah and Goonur were distracted by all the singing and dancing, and forgot about the firesticks. Seeing his chance, Beeargah grabbed one stick from the scrub and the other stick from the *comebee*. He rubbed the two sticks together and set fire to a nearby patch of grass. Goonur and Bootoolgah saw the fire and realized that Beeargah had stolen their firesticks. They tried to chase him, but he was too fast. Beeargah flew from patch to patch, lighting fires in the grass.

Goonur and Bootoolgah gave up. "We are sorry," they said. "We should not have kept this gift a secret from our brothers and sisters." The other animals forgave them, and from that night on everyone ate delicious, cooked fish.

Glossary

ancestor A person from whom one is descended

breeder A person who raises certain types of animals for sale

denomination An organized religious group within a faith

discus A heavy, plate-shaped object thrown in sports competitions

diversity Variety

fiber A thread-like piece of plant material

javelin A light spear thrown in sports competitions

mammal A warm-blooded animal that gives birth to live babies.

marinade A mix of spices, vinegar, oil or wine, poured on meat, fish, and vegetables to add flavor

opal A mineral used as a gemstone

orally By word of mouth

reed The hollow stalk of a tall grass

replica An exact copy of an object

ritual A religious ceremony in which steps must be followed in a certain order

sacred Having special religious significance

suburban Describing a residential area outside a city

supernatural Spirits and forces that cannot be explained by science

tram A streetcar

wake-boarding A water sport similar to waterskiing except using a single board instead of two skis. The term wake comes from the waves, or wake, that boats create as they move through water.

watercolor Paint mixed with water, not oil

World War II A war fought by countries around the world from 1939 to 1945

Index

1 2 3 4 5 6 7 8 9 0   Printed in the USA   0 9 8 7 6 5 4 3 2